Crochet Christmas Ornaments

Easy Crochet Christmas Ornaments That'll Cozy up Your Tree

Copyright © 2023

All rights reserved.

DEDICATION

The author and publisher have provided this e-book to you for your personal use only. You may not make this e-book publicly available in any way. Copyright infringement is against the law. If you believe the copy of this e-book you are reading infringes on the author's copyright, please notify the publisher at: https://us.macmillan.com/piracy

Contents

Snow Globe Ornaments 1

Stocking Ornaments 4

Christmas Light Ornaments 19

Little Christmas Mouse 23

Christmas Tree Ornament 31

Bells Christmas Ornament 37

Retro Ornament Garland 44

Snowman Ornament 53

Snow Globe Ornaments

Materials:

– Bernat Super Value Yarn in Cool Blue, Berry Red, and White. You could also use Grey, Black, Brown, or Dark Blue for the base.

– Size H Crochet Hook

– Small tapestry needle or sewing needle

– Christmas Buttons!

Pattern:

Magic Ring, chain 1 and make 10 SC in ring, join to first SC, chain 1

Round 2: 2 SC in each stitch around, join, chain 1

Round 3: 2 SC in first stitch, SC in next, repeat around, join, chain 1 (30 SC)

Round 4: 2 SC in first stitch, SC in next 4, repeat around, join, chain 1 (36 SC)

Round 5: SC in each stitch around (36 SC)

add in red yarn (or black/brown/grey), join, chain 1

Row 6: SC in first 7, chain 1, turn

Row 7: 2 SC in first, SC in next 5, 2 SC in last, chain 1, turn

Row 8-9: SC in each stitch across, chain 1, turn

Fasten off and weave in ends.

Use tapestry needle to sew on cute Christmas buttons to the center of your snowglobes! Don't forget the snowflake buttons! Those are a must.

Stocking Ornaments

Materials:

-Lion Brand 24/7 Cotton in Red and White

-Size E crochet hook

-Tapestry needle

*Do not join rounds, places a stitch marker in the first stitch of the round and move it up with each round

Pattern:

Striped Stocking:

With white, make a magic ring, Ch 1, 6 Sc in ring (6)

Round 2: 2 Sc in each around (12)

Round 3: 2 Sc, Sc in next, repeat around (18)

Rounds 4-6: Sc in each around (18)

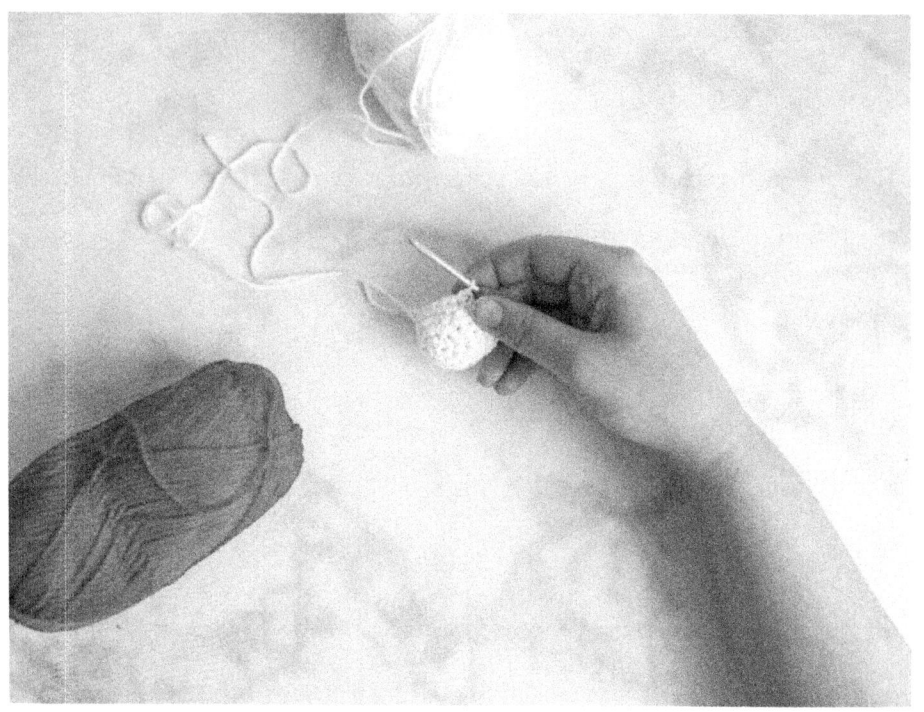

*Color change to Red

Rounds 7-8: Sc in each around (18)

*Color change to White

Crochet Christmas Ornaments

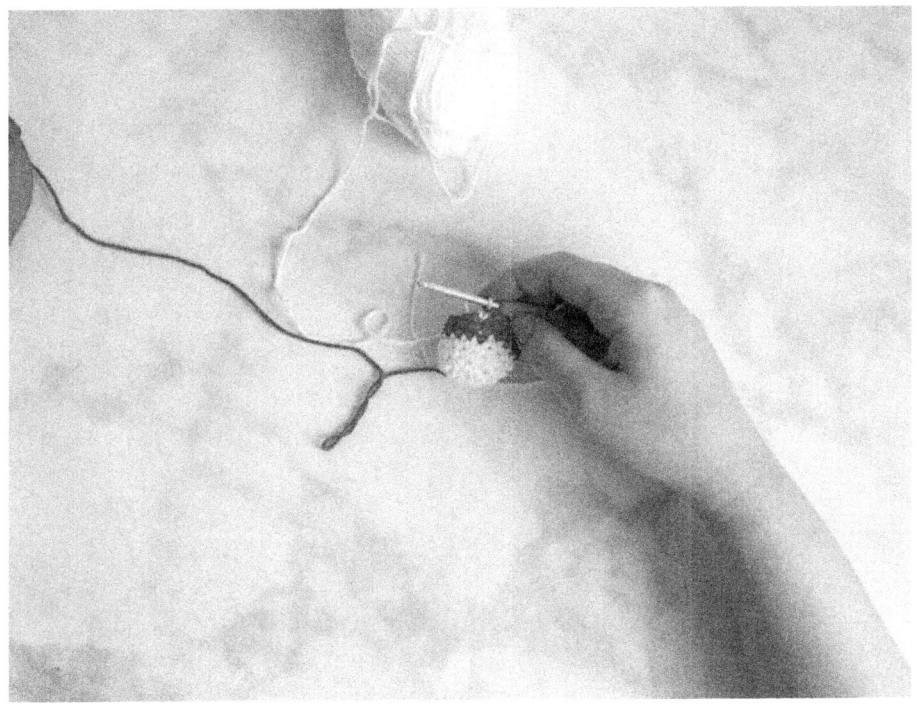

Rounds 9-10: Sc in each around (18)

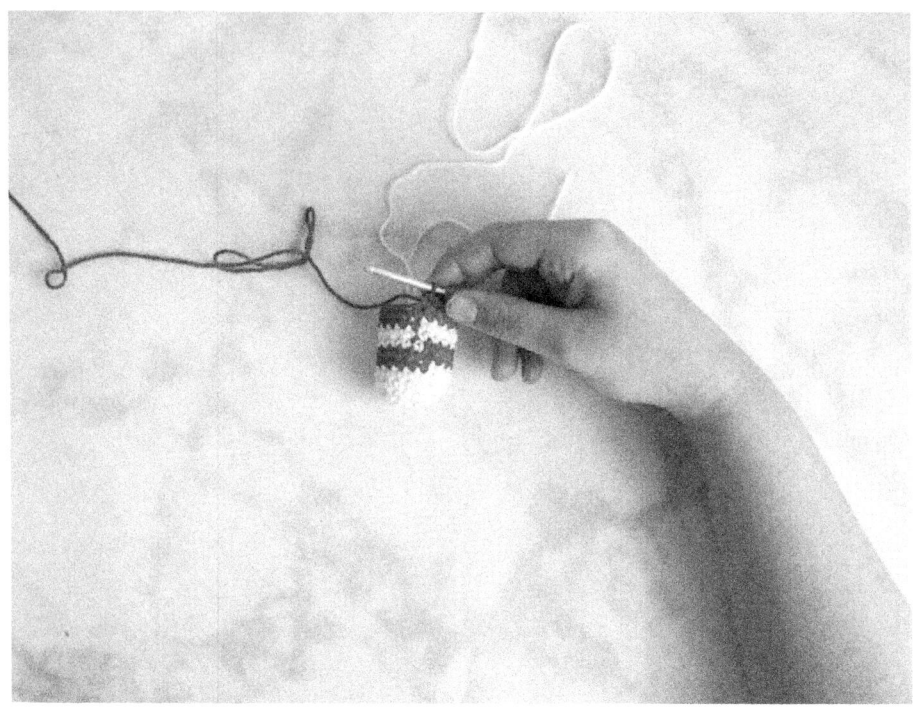

*Color change to Red

Rounds 11-12: Sc in each around (18)

Crochet Christmas Ornaments

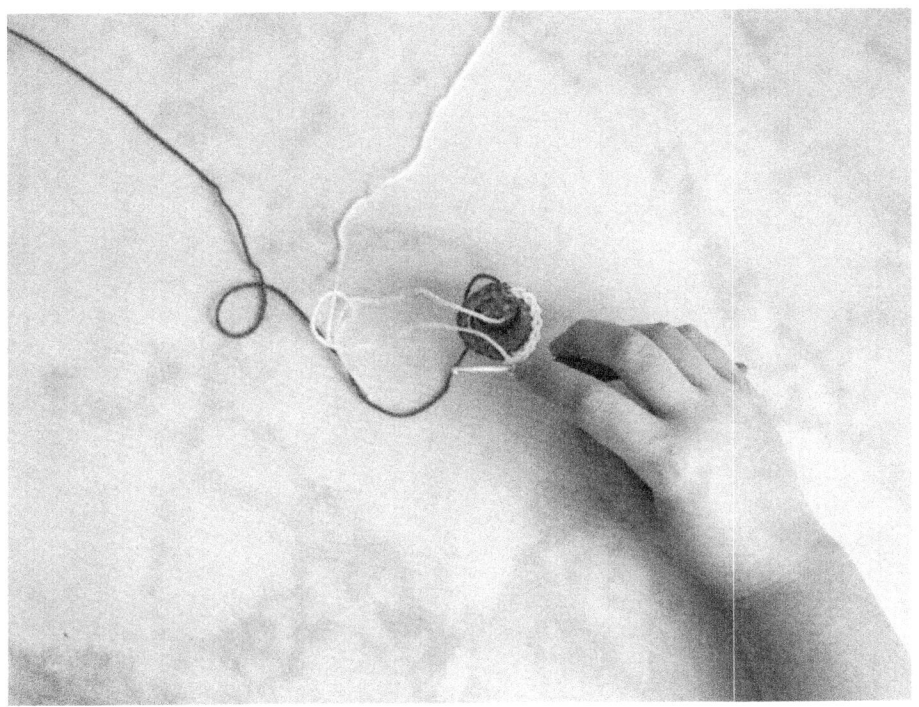

Round 13: Sc in next 9 sts, Ch 1, turn (9)

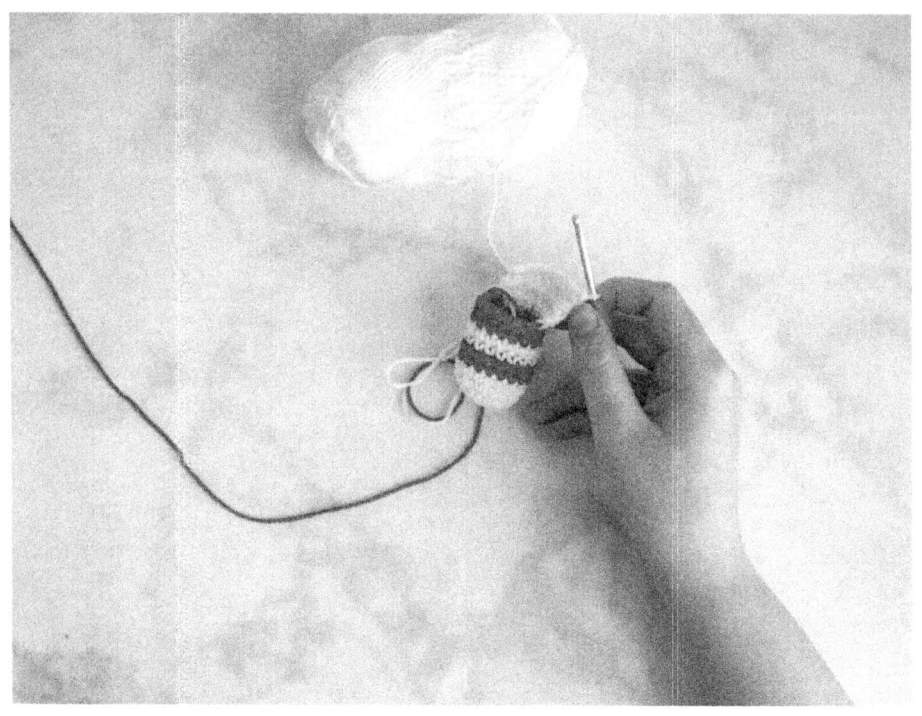

Rounds 14-17: Sc in each across, Ch 1, turn (9)

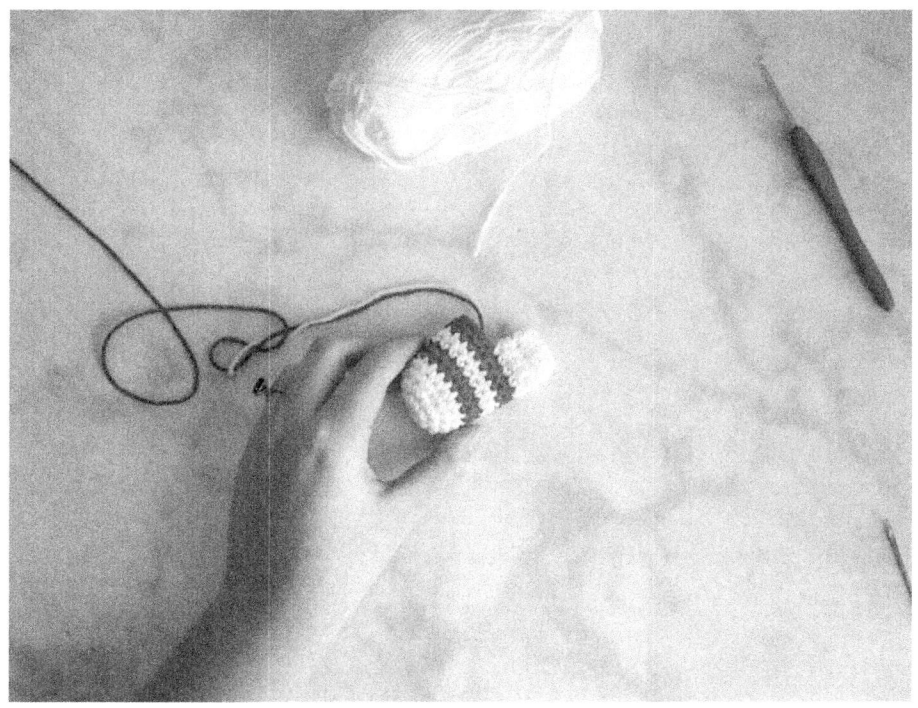

Round 18: Pick up Red yarn from Round 12, Sc around the stocking and heel as pictured (18)

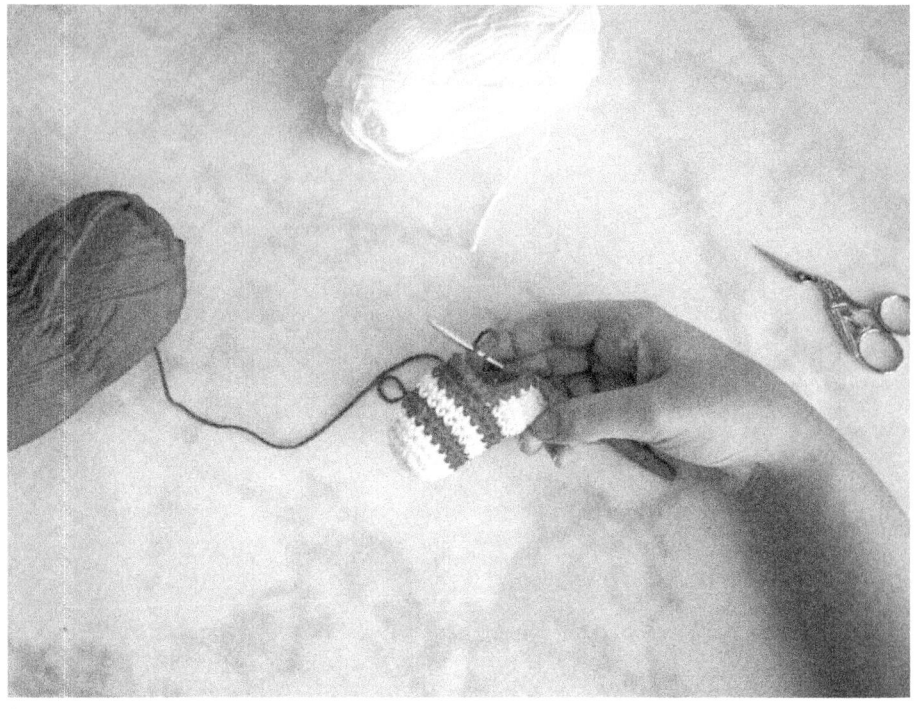

Round 19: Sc in each around (18)

*Color change to White

Rounds 20-21: Sc in each around (18)

*Color change to Red

Rounds 22-23: Sc in each around (18)

*Color change to White

Rounds 24-25: Sc in each around (18)

*Color change to Red

Rounds 26-27: Sc in each around (18)

*Color change to White

Rounds 28-29: Sc in each around (18)

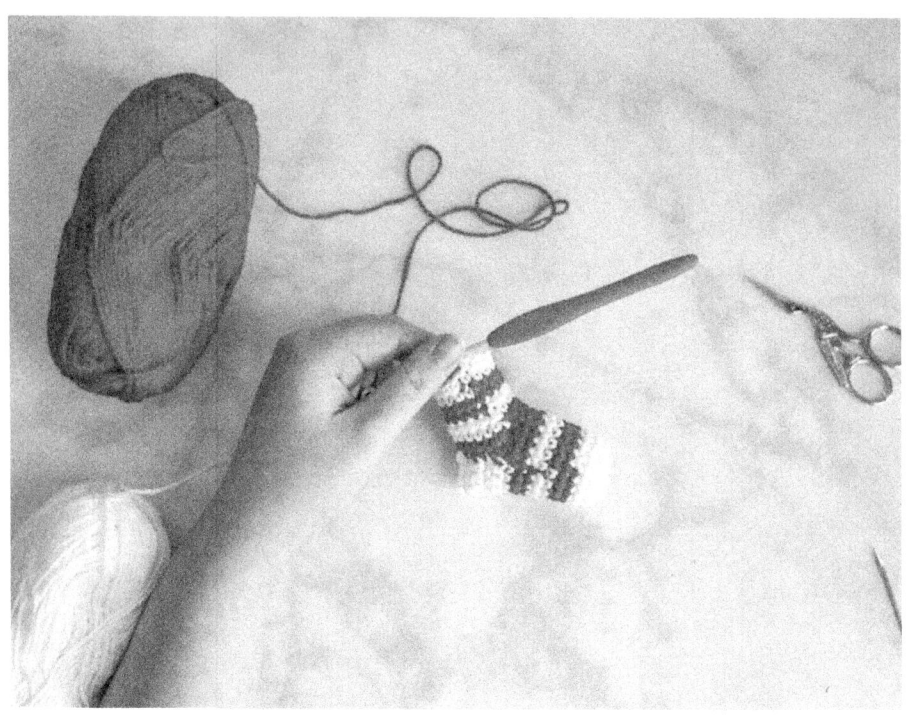

Finish off, weave ends, join red yarn to the side above the heel, Ch 8, sl st in same st where you joined yarn, finish off and weave ends

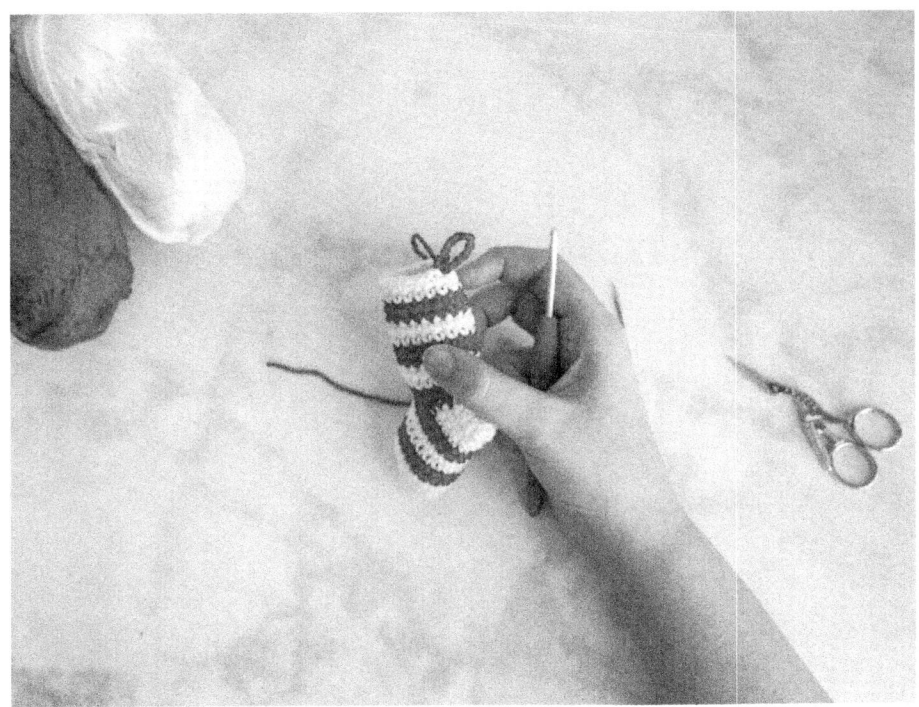

Solid Stocking:

With white, make a magic ring, Ch 1, 6 Sc in ring (6)

Round 2: 2 Sc in each around (12)

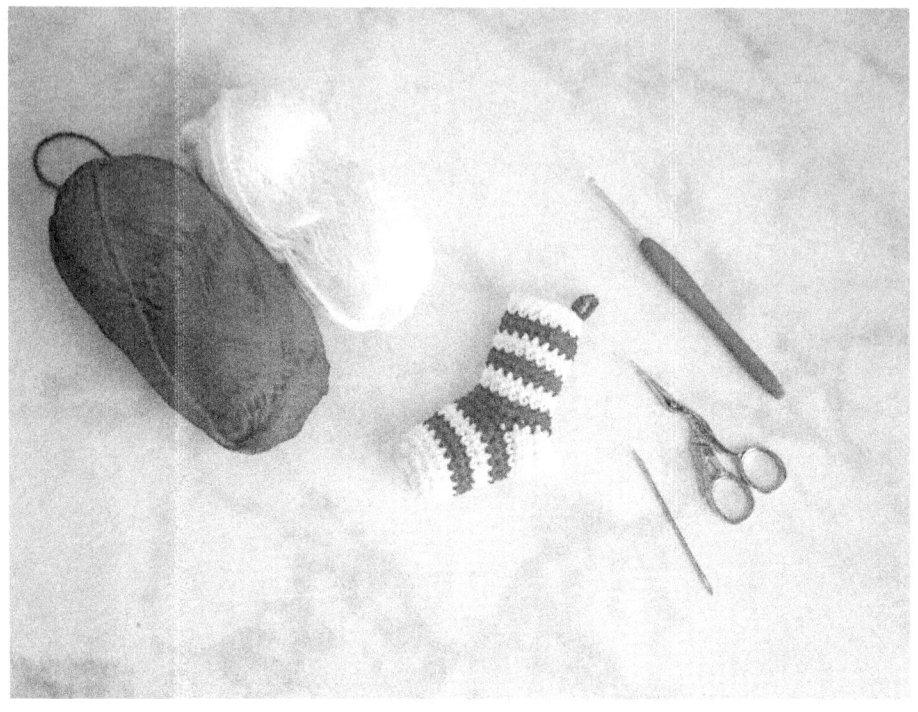

Round 3: 2 Sc, Sc in next, repeat around (18)

Rounds 4-6: Sc in each around (18)

*Color change to Red

Rounds 7-12: Sc in each around (18)

*Color change to White — don't finish off Red yarn

Round 13: Sc in next 9 sts, Ch 1, turn (9)

Rounds 14-17: Sc in each across, Ch 1, turn (9)

Finish off leaving a long tail for sewing, using a tapestry needle sew the heel closed as pictured

Round 18: Pick up Red yarn from Round 12, Sc around the stocking and heel as pictured (18)

Rounds 19-27: Sc in each around (18)

*Color change to White

Rounds 28-29: Sc in each around (18)

Round 30: Sc in next 7, Ch 8, Sc in next 13 sts of the round, sl st in next, finish off and weave all ends

Christmas Light Ornaments

Materials:

– Lion Brand 24/7 Cotton in silver, tangerine, red, grass, yellow, and sky

– Size E 3.25 crochet hook

– Tapestry needle

– Polyfil stuffing

Pattern:

Bulb:

*Do not join rounds for the bulb, use a stitch marker to place in the last st of each round, and move up as you complete each round

Begin with chosen color and make a magic ring, Ch 1, work 6 Sc inside ring (6)

Round 2: 2 Sc in each around (12)

Round 3: Sc in each around (12)

Round 4: 2 Sc in first, Sc in next, repeat around (18)

Round 5: Sc in each around (18)

Round 6: 2 Sc in first, Sc in next 2, repeat around (24)

Rounds 7-9: Sc in each around (24)

Round 10: 2 Sc in first, Sc in next 3, repeat around (30)

Round 11: Sc in each around (30)

Round 12: Sc decrease, Sc in next 3, repeat around (24)

Round 13: Sc decrease, Sc in next 2, repeat around (18)

Round 14: Sc in each around (18)

Round 15: Sc decrease, Sc in next, repeat around, finish off, weave ends (12)

– Stuff with polyfil stuffing

Topper:

Begin with silver and amke a magic ring, Ch 1, work 6 Sc inside ring, sl st to join, Ch 1 (6)

Round 2: 2 Sc in each around, sl st to join, Ch 1 (12)

Round 3: Sc in back loops only in each around, sl st to join, Ch 1 (12)

Round 3: Sc in each around, sl st to join, finish off leaving a long tail for sewing (12)

– Sew connector to bulb opening, weave all ends

Little Christmas Mouse

Abbreviations:

ch = chain

st = stitch or stitches

ss = slipstitch

sc = single crochet (US), double crochet (UK)

dc = double crochet (US), treble crochet (UK)

tog = together

sc2tog = decrease by working two sc together

FLO = work in front loop only

FO = fasten off

Approximate size: 5cm/2" long without tail.

General instructions:

Work in rounds unless otherwise stated and do not join rounds unless told to. Use a stitch marker to mark the start of a round - a small piece of different coloured yarn placed under the stitch at the start of the round will do. To start a round, you can use the magic ring method, but I prefer to ch 2, and work the appropriate number of sc into 1st ch. If you work the sc over the tail of yarn as well you can use that to pull the hole tight.

When changing from one colour of yarn to another work the stitch before the change until there are two loops left on the hook. Then use the new colour for the final yarn over hook and pull through.

Work through both loops of stitches unless otherwise indicated.

Materials:

Small amounts of double knitting or worsted weight yarn:

A natural fur colour for the head and tail.

Two colours of yarn, such as red and green, for the body.

Small amount of black yarn to embroider eyes.

Small length of cotton yarn.

Small amount of stuffing.

3.5mm (E) hook.

Tapestry needle.

Pattern:

Start with natural fur colour yarn.

Round 1: Ch 2, work 4 sc into 1st ch - 4 st.

Round 2: [2 sc in next st, sc in next st] 2 times - 6 st.

Round 3: [2 sc in next st, sc in next 2 st] 2 times - 8 st.

Round 4: [2 sc in next st, sc in next 3 st] 2 times - 10 st.

Round 5: Sc in each st around – 10 st.

Round 6: [2 sc in next st, sc in next 4 st] 2 times - 12 st.

Round 7: Sc in next 6 st, [ear, in FLO of next st: ss, ch 2, 5 dc, ch 2, ss], sc in next 3 st, [ear as before], sc in next st – 12 st (counting each ear as one st).

Round 8: Sc in each st around, working into the back loop behind each ear – 12 st.

Stuff head and use black yarn to sew eyes.

Change to first yarn colour for body.

Round 9: [2 sc in next st, sc in next st] 3 times, sc in next 6 st – 15 st.

Round 10: [2 sc in next st, sc in next 4 st] 3 times – 18 st.

Change to second yarn colour for body.

Round 11: Sc in each st around – 18 st.

Change to first yarn colour for body.

Round 12: [Sc in next 2 st, 2 sc in next st, sc in next 3 st] 3 times – 21 st.

Change to second yarn colour for body.

Round 13: Sc in each st around – 21 st.

Change to first yarn colour for body.

Round 14 - 15: (2 rounds) Sc in each st around – 21 st.

Change to natural fur colour yarn.

Round 16: [Sc2tog, sc in next 5 st] 2 times, sc2tog, sc in next 2 st, [tail: ss in next st, ch 20, miss ch next to hook, ss 19, ss back into original st], sc in next 2 st – 18 st.

Round 17: Sc2tog 2 times, sc in next 6 st, sc2tog 4 times – 12 st.

Round 18: Sc2tog 6 times – 6 st.

FO, leaving a length of yarn. Using cotton yarn, sew a loop behind the head if you want to hang your mouse as a decoration. Finish stuffing and sew up bottom of mouse neatly - if you stuff the body well it will sit up nicely.

Christmas Tree Ornament

Materials:

1 pack Lion Brand Yarn Bonbons in Beach (100% Cotton yarn; fingering weight), which comes with 8 mini skeins. – You need less

than a skein of green, black & red to complete the ornament.

US size F (3.75 mm) crochet hook

scissors

tapestry needle

poly-fil

straight pins with faux pearl heads

scrap ribbon

sewing needle & thread

Abbreviations & Terms

magic ring – an adjustable starting round. Here's a tutorial.

sc – single crochet

rep from * – repeat the instructions follow- ing the asterisk as directed

ch – chain

rnd – round

(X sts) – X is the number of sts that are now in the rnd

sl – slip

blsc – sc into the back of the ch. Here's a tutorial.

blsc2 in next st – back loop single crochet two times in same st

sc2 in next st – sc 2 times in same st

(Y rnds) – Y is the number of times you work the rnd

hdc – half double crochet

Gauge & Dimensions: Approx. 19 sc & 23 rows over 4 inches. Finished tree measures 3.5" tall.

Pattern:

Make Tree Top

rnd 1. Using green yarn, form a magic ring & sc 6 into ring. Pull tail to tighten loop.

rnd 2. ch1, *blsc 1, blsc 2 in next st; rep from * 3 times. (9 sts)

rnd 3. blsc 9.

rnd 4. *blsc 2, blsc 2 in next st; rep from * 3 times. (12 sts)

rnd 5. blsc 12.

rnd 6. *blsc 3, blsc 2 in next st; rep from * 3 times. (15 sts)

rnd 7. blsc 15.

rnd 8. *blsc 4, blsc 2 in next st; rep from * 3 times. (18 sts)

rnd 9. blsc 18.

rnd 10. *blsc 5, blsc 2 in next st; rep from * 3 times. (21 sts)

rnd 11. blsc 21.

rnd 12. *blsc 6, blsc 2 in next st; rep from * 3 times. (24 sts)

rnd 13. blsc 24.

rnd 14. *blsc 7, blsc 2 in next st; rep from * 3 times. (27 sts)

rnd 15. blsc 27, sl to join.

Break yarn and draw tail through last loop to secure.

Make Tree Trunk

rnd 1. Using black yarn, form a magic ring & sc 6 into ring. Pull tail to tighten loop.

rnd 2. ch1, sc twice in each st, sl to join. (12 sts)

rnd 3. blsc 12.

rnds 4-5. sc 12. (2 rnds)

rnd 6. Using green yarn, ch 2 (counts as hdc), hdc in same ch, *hdc 2 in next st; rep from * 11 times, sl to join. (24 sts)

Break yarn and draw tail through last loop to secure.

Finishing

Sew trunk to top of tree, stuffing as you go. Weave in all ends. Finish by using red scrap yarn to create a garland and "decorate" the tree with straight pins.

Bells Christmas Ornament

Materials:

Sport or DK weight yarn in Red and White colors

4mm crochet hook

Fiberfill

Large beads or jingle bells

Ribbon Bow

Tapestry needle

Abbreviations

ch = chain

sc = single crochet

st = stitch

sl st = slip stitch

beg = beginning

(C1) = color 1

(C2) = color 2

Notes

Beg ch does not count as st.

Less than 30 yards required for this pattern.

Pattern:

(Make 2)

With (C1), Make a magic ring.

Row 1: (work in rows) ch 1, 4 sc into the ring, turn. (4 sts)

Row 2: ch 1, 2 sc in first st, sc in each of next 2 sts, 2 sc in last st, turn. (6 sts)

Row 3: ch 1, sc in each st across, turn. (6 sts)

Row 4: repeat row 3. (6 sts)

Row 5: ch 1, 2 sc in first st, sc in each of next 4 sts, 2 sc in last st, turn. (8 sts)

Row 6: ch 1, sc in each st across, turn. (8 sts)

Row 7: repeat row 6.

Row 8: ch 1, 2 sc in first st, sc in each of next 6 sts, 2 sc in last st, turn. (10 sts)

Row 9: ch 1, sc in each st across, turn. (10 sts)

Row 10: repeat row 9.

Row 11: ch 1, 2 sc in first st, sc in each of next 8 sts, 2 sc in last st, turn. (12 sts)

Row 12: ch 1, 2 sc in first st, sc in each of next 10 sts, 2 sc in last st, turn. (14 sts)

Row 13: ch 1, 2 sc in first st, sc in each of next 12 sts, 2 sc in last st, turn. (16 sts)

Row 14: ch 1, sc in each st across, turn. (16 sts)

Row 15: (sc around the edge) crochet sc around the edge. 3 sc in corner st (at the magic ring on the top and corner sts on two sides of the bell). Fasten off and weave the ends.

Joining two pieces together

Holding two pieces together, with (C1) begin at the 2nd st of 3 sc at the top of the bell. Crochet sc around the edge to joining two pieces. Crochet 3 sc in the second st of each 3 sts (each corner st) to get smooth edging. Add fiberfill while joining. Don't forget to fill lightly. sl st to the first st.

After joining two pieces together, crochet ch 30 or 40 and sl st to the first st (made a loop). Fasten off and weave the ends.

Edging

Start at the top of the bell. With (C2), crochet slip stitch (sl st) around the previous round. Fasten off and weave the end.

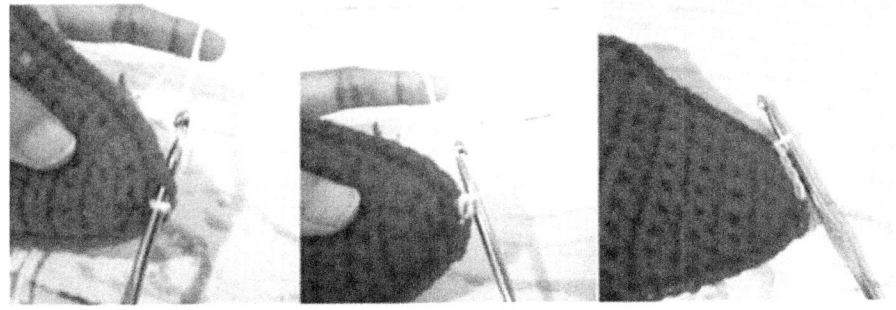

How to crochet slip stitch around the edge? Insert the hook in a st of the previous row at the top of the bell. yarn over, pull up a loop, *insert the hook in next st, yarn over, pull up a loop through st and the loop on the hook; repeat * to around the edge, Fasten off and weave the ends.

Retro Ornament Garland

Materials:

Worsted Weight Yarn

Size I (5.50 mm) Crochet Hook

Wooden Beads

Gloss Craft Paint

Yarn Needle

Ornament 1 Pattern

Special Stitches:

Half-Treble Crochet (htrc) – Yarn over twice, insert hook into work, yarn over (four loops on hook), yarn over and draw through two loops (three loops on hook), yarn over and draw through all loops.

Pattern:

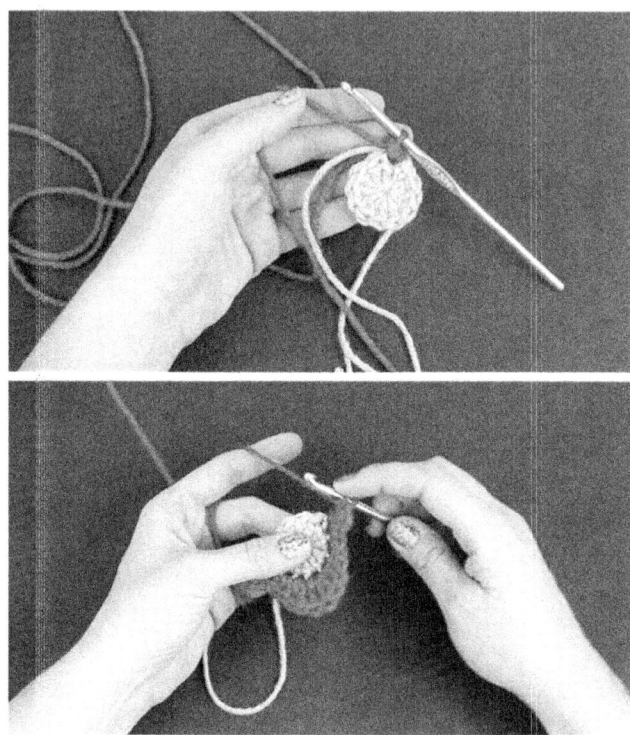

Round 1: Start with a magic loop, ch 3 and work 11 dc in the magic loop. Pull tail to tighten circle, slip stitch to join. Finish off weave in ends.

Round 2: Join new color, ch 1, (sc, ch 2, trc, ch 2, sc) all in same stitch,

*2 hdc in next st, (dc, htrc) in next st, 3 trc in next st, (htrc, dc) in next st, 2 hdc in next st,** (sc, ch 2, trc, ch 2, sc) all in next st, repeat from * to **, sl st to join. Finish off and weave in ends.

Next we will attach a little tassel to the bottom of the ornament.

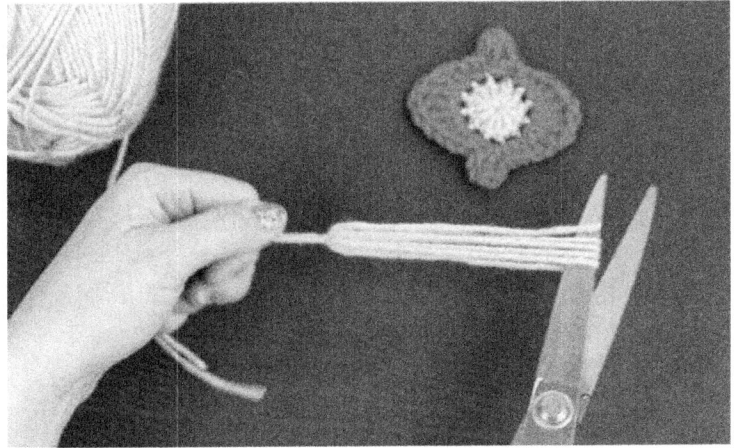

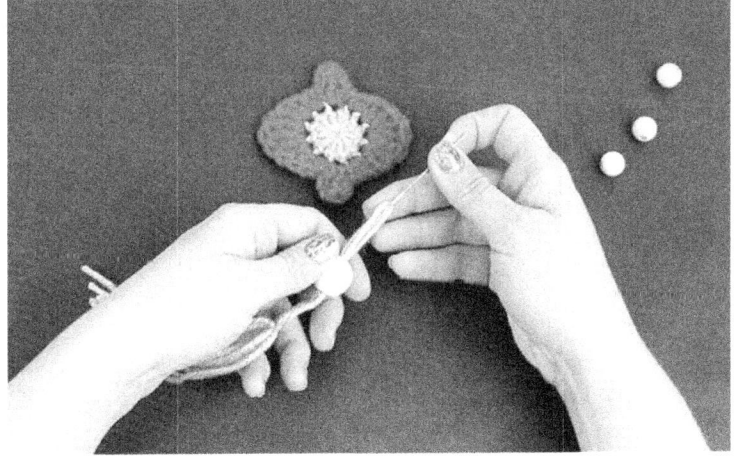

Start by wrapping the yarn around your fingers four or five times. Cut off a length of yarn, thread through the top of the loops you just made and double knot it. Cut through the bottom of the loops. Use the yarn needle to thread a bead or two onto the top of the tassel. Tie onto the bottom of the ornament and cut off excess.

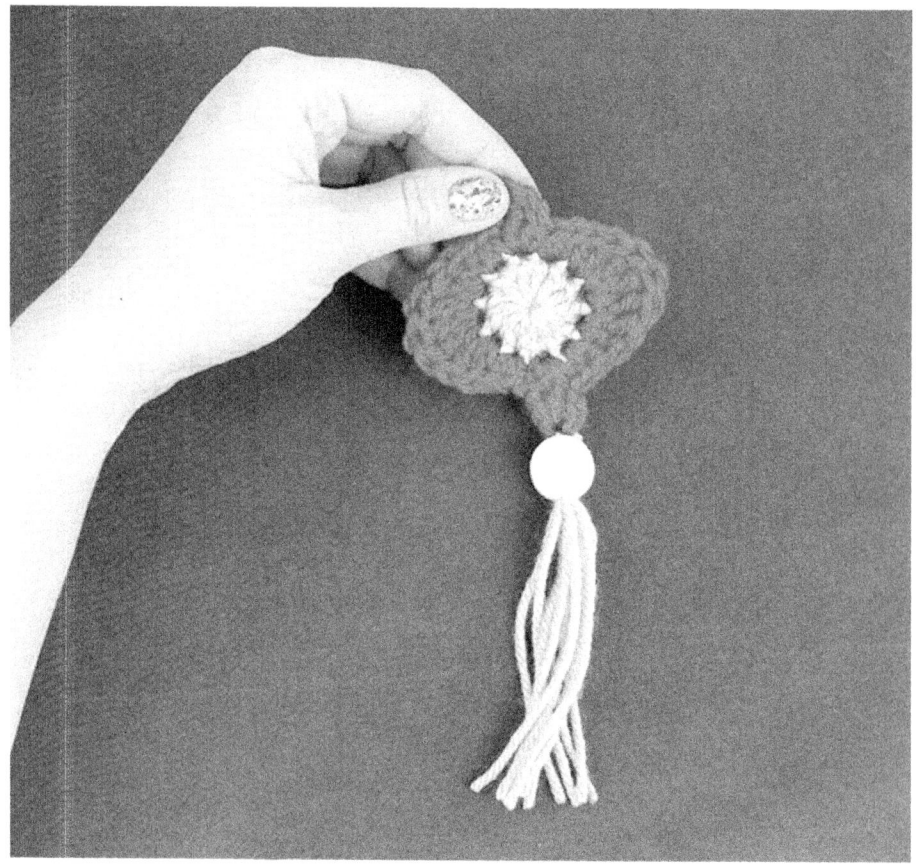

Ornament 2 Pattern

For this ornament, you will crochet three circles and stitch them together.

Circle 1

Round 1: Start with magic loop, ch 3, 11 dc in magic loop, pull to tighten, sl st to join.

Round 2: Ch 3, dc in same st, 2 dc in each st around, sl st to join. Finish off, weave in ends.

Circle 2

Round 1: Start with magic loop, ch 3, 11 dc in magic loop, pull to tighten, sl st to join.

Round 2: Ch 1, sc in same st, sc, 2 sc, * sc, sc, 2 sc, repeat from * twice, sl st to join. Do not finish off.

Using the same yarn, crochet through the bottom two stitches of circle one. When the two circles are securely attached, finish off and weave in ends.

Circle 3

Round 1: Start with magic loop, ch 3, 11 dc in magic loop, pull to tighten, sl st to join. Stitch through bottom two stitches of Circle 2. Finish off, weave in ends.

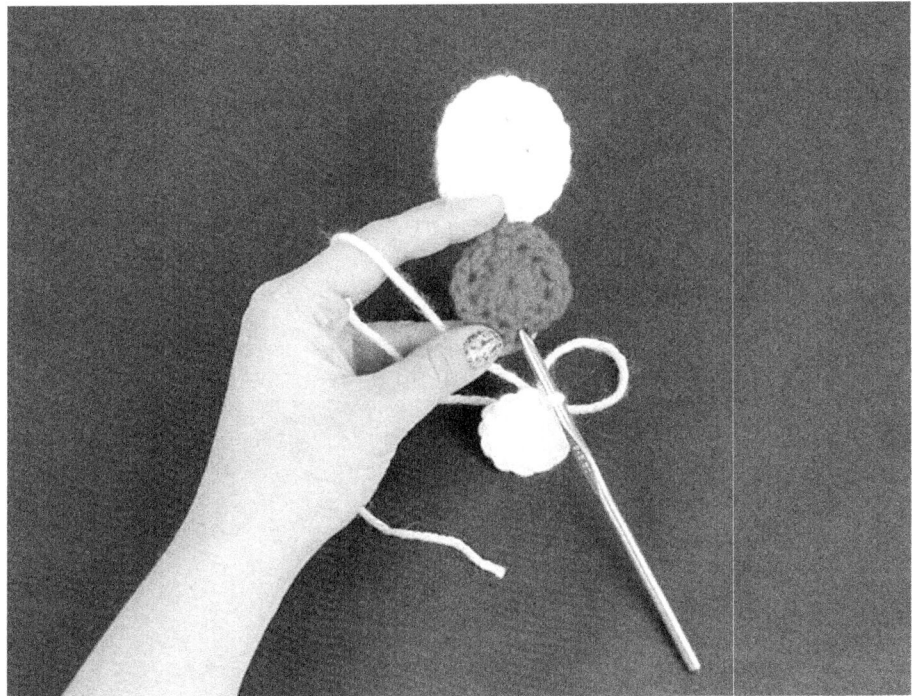

And that's it for Ornament 2!

Ornament 3 Pattern

Round 1: Start with magic loop, ch 3, 11 dc in magic loop, pull to tighten, sl st to join.

Round 2: Ch 3, dc in same st, 2 dc in each st around, sl st to join. Finish off, weave in ends.

Round 3: Join new color, ch 1, sc in same st, sc in each of next 6 stitches, hdc, (hdc, dc), (htrc, trc, htrc), (dc, hdc), hdc, sc in each of next 7 sts, hdc, (hdc, dc), (htrc, trc, htrc), (dc, hdc), hdc, sl st to join. Finish off, weave in ends.

Snowman Ornament

Materials:

Worsted weight yarn in the following colors- white, black, brown, green, red, and orange (you only need a small amount of each so this is a great project for using up scraps, the red and green can be replaced with any color you want)

G crochet hook

stuffing

yarn needle

2 small buttons (about 1/4"-3/8")

sewing needle

sewing thread

small piece of crochet thread

Pattern:

Body

with white yarn

Round 1: in mr, ch 1, 6 sc (6 sc)

Round 2: 2 sc in each stitch (12 sc)

Round 3: [1 sc in first stitch, 2 sc in next] repeat around (18 sc)

Round 4: [1 sc in first 2 stitches, 2 sc in next] repeat around (24 sc)

Round 5: [1 sc in first 3 stitches, 2 sc in next]repeat around (30 sc)

Rounds 6-9: 1 sc in each stitch (30 sc)

Round 10: [1 sc in first 3 stitches, sc2tog] repeat around (24 sc)

Round 11: [1 sc in first 2 stitches, sc2tog] repeat around, change to white yarn at the end of round (18 sc)

begin stuffing and continue adding stuffing as needed to the end

Round 12: [1 sc in first stitch, sc2tog] repeat around, change to tan yarn at the end of the row (12 sc)

Round 13: 2 sc in each stitch (24 sc)

Round 14-16: 1 sc in each stitch (24 sc)

Round 17: [1 sc in first 2 stitches, sc2tog] repeat around (18 sc)

Round 18:[1 sc in first stitch, sc2tog] repeat around (12 sc)

Round 19: sc2tog, repeat around (6 sc)

Finish off

Hat

start with black yarn

Round 1: in mr, ch 1, 6 sc (6 sc)

Round 2: 2 sc in each stitch (12 sc)

Round 3: [1 sc in first stitch, 2 sc in next] repeat around (18 sc)

Round 4: sc in blo of each stitch around (18 sc)

Round 5: 1 sc in each stitch around, at the end of round change to red yarn (18 sc)

Round 6: 1 sc in each stitch around (18 sc)

Round 7: 1 sc in each stitch around, at the end of round change to black yarn (18 sc)

Round 8: 2 sc in each stitch around (36 sc)

Finish off leaving long end for sewing

Scarf

the scarf is made in 2 pieces, the long piece wraps around the neck, the short piece fold over that piece to make the scarf ends

with green yarn

ch 21

sc in each stitch (20 sc)

finish off leaving long end for sewing

ch 13

sc in each stitch (12 sc)

finish off and weave in ends

Arms

with brown yarn, make 2

ch 7, slip stitch in first 3, ch 4, slip stitch in those 4 and the first 4

Assembly

Stitch the hat to the top of the head, you may want it to be slightly tilted

Fold the short scarf piece over the long scarf piece, wrap the long piece around his neck and stitch together in the back, make sure the small piece is where you want it and stitch through that piece to secure

Stitch the arms to the sides of the body, just under the scarf

With thread and sewing needle sew the buttons to the front of the body

Stitch the face with black and orange yarn

Attach the crochet thread to the top of the head and tie in a loop for hanging, pull so that the knot is inside of the hat

Now you have a cute little snowman ornament to hang on your tree.

Printed in Great Britain
by Amazon